WOEBEGONE POETRY WRITTEN WITH MY FATHER'S PEN

Terri Ricardo

BookLeaf Publishing

India | USA | UK

Presentation by *BookLeaf Publishing*

Web: www.bookleafpub.com

E-mail: info@bookleafpub.com

ISBN: 9789363303126

First edition 2024

This book is dedicated to my father

John.V.Ricardo

2/11/1951—10/15/2023

ACKNOWLEDGMENT

This book would not have come to life without the unwavering support of those who walked beside me through the journey of loss and the healing process of setting grief to words.

Foremost, I wish to honor the memory of my father, whose love and presence continue to inspire me. These poems are born of his spirit, and to him, I owe my deepest gratitude.

To my family, especially my sisters—thank you for being my companions in remembrance. Your shared strength, laughter, and love have been a constant source of comfort.

To my friends, thank you for listening, allowing me space to grieve, and offering the kindness that gave me the courage to write.

I am profoundly grateful to everyone who encouraged me to capture these memories in poetry, helping me honor the enduring love that remains even after loss. Your faith in me has been my guiding light.

A special thanks to BookLeaf Publishing for this opportunity and to Roosha Debnath, who went above and beyond with her guidance and support throughout the editing process. Your commitment and care have been invaluable, and I am truly grateful.

And to you, the reader—thank you for sharing in these memories. May these poems offer you solace and remind us all of the resilience found in love, remembrance, and the journey of healing.

With heartfelt gratitude,
Terri Ricardo

PREFACE

Grief has a way of rewriting everything we think we know about loss. It changes us, humbling us and revealing depths of love and pain we never imagined possible. For years, I watched friends lose their parents, offering them my heartfelt condolences yet never truly grasping the enormity of their loss. And then, one day, I joined them on this unfamiliar, unchosen path when my father passed away.

The poems you hold in this book are the story of that journey—a series of attempts to make sense of the heartbreak, to reach out and touch the past, to hold onto someone who is both everywhere and nowhere. In these pages, I tried to capture the echoes of my father, the tender memories, the laughter, and even the unanswered questions. I wrote with his pen, almost as if doing so could somehow pull him back, just for a moment, into this world.

Writing became a way to converse with him again, as though he might hear my words through a wind phone or leave me a sign in a cardinal's flight. Each poem is an exploration, a seeking. There's the searching for meaning in his belongings, the surprise of finding humor amid sorrow, and the quiet of the nights when memories rise unbidden and sleep seems impossible.

In these verses, you may find something familiar if you, too, are grieving—an acknowledgment that grief isn't a linear process but a vast landscape of memories, doubts, and ultimately, love. There are no clear answers here but perhaps a shared comfort. I hope that these words remind you, as they did me, that even in loss, our loved ones leave us with something precious: the indelible impact of their lives, a legacy of love, and moments that live on.

Thank you for joining me in this journey of remembrance. May these pages be a small beacon of understanding and a reminder that we never grieve alone.

With love and remembrance,
Terri Ricardo

Table of Contents

Gone

I got that phone call; he was gone.
Headed to the nursing home to say goodbye.
My father's husband spoke with a slight drawl.
Rubbed my eyes, tried not to cry.
His mouth hung open, but there was no sound.
He was wearing only his hospital gown.
I was hoping the staff was wrong.
Maybe he will jump up and ask what's going on?
It was true my Dad had passed away.
What a horrible day.
Now what?
Do I just go home and follow societal norms?

Higher Power

2

First I cried.
Then I angrily expostulated with God on his decision to take my father.
It was like Saint Peregrine couldn't be bothered.
This devastating loss makes me doubt this higher power.
Was my father praying to nothing in his final hour?

Death Certificate

3

Getting the death certificate in the mail makes it
feel so official.
Feels like my heart received a cold chisel.
Why is this piece of paper so gloomy?
Shouldn't it talk about my Dad's beauty?

Check Back In A Year

Grief is like a series of natural disasters, that hit
you at random.
The whole time will heal things,
I can't even fathom.
Longing for the day when I can look through
photos without crying.
God knows, my sisters and I keep trying.
Check back in a year; maybe we will get there.

King

5

When you leave behind holy water, rosary
beads, and a Jesus statue, it shows your faith was
strong and true.
Your home movies are Oscar worthy.
They will forever be a treasure of your journey.
Your paintings should have been world
renowned.
King of Pride, you have now been crowned.
Lead the parade in heaven, and be proud.
You left us with so much after all.

Moon Cake

6

I speak for grief, looking up at the stars.
Are the angels hiding behind the moon cake?
Trying to figure out who they are,
Do they know we want them here in human
form?
Will they wipe our tears at night?
Or visit us in our dreams to help us ride out the
storm?
Or will the current carry this feeling of loss
away?

I Believe in the Moon

Looking out the window, trying to translate the
language of the moon.
I believe the moon says who needs enemies,
when you have grief.
I believe it says, I'm sending you a kiss from
your father on my moonbeams.
I believe the moon is telling me, he is always
with you,
sweet dreams…

Damn the sky for being so big

I want to find the entrance to heaven to visit, not
stay.
I want to hug those who have gone before me.
I want to console them and pray.

I would elaborate to them on the void they left,
and my utter bereft.
I would ask what happens when your soul
embarks,
Do you see light or dark?

Unique Snowflake

9

We know your soul is in the unique snowflakes
that touch the ground.
You would never be a boring star in the sky.
The pangs of grief have me trying to find
symbols and signs from you in the runaround.
No matter how much time passes, I'll never be
ready to say goodbye.

Memory

I am offering this memory, for I have nothing
else to give.
You brought us on the ferry.
Sun shining down, wind blowing our hair.
You even came prepared.
You gave us our backgammon game to play.
You knew this would occupy us most of the way.
The destination was P town.
We did not even give it a second thought.
We did not care that our Dad was gay.

Wind Phone

I called you from a wind phone today.
I wanted to hear you say hello.
I wanted you to tell me you were okay.
They must have not paid the bill.
I did not hear you.
Were you on the other end just being still?
I wanted to reminisce about your photo in the
paper with the Buffalo.
Could you please call me back?
I just want to hear you say hello.

Heavy Cross to Bear

Your birthday was the other day; it was a heavy cross to bear.

Every holiday is just a reminder you are no longer here.

Not having you to share milestones with is just depressing.

I hope you're watching from up above and taking notes.

Because when I get there, I will ask a lot of questions to see if you were paying attention.

Hoarder

My father was a hoarder but clean and
organized.
Still, it took four months to clean out his home,
to my surprise.
Who gets to keep his ridiculous cowboy hat?
Finding his weed stash gave us a laugh.
No matter the size of the home or how much is
in it,
Going through everything won't untangle the
grief that just continues.

Random Words On A Page

Massa
Birch trees
Freddy
Beach
Painting
Nurse
Photos
Music
Cardinals
Recipes
Father
Son
Brother
Husband
Friend
Plaids
Artist
Grandfather

I Haven't Seen A Cardinal

15

I have not seen a cardinal since your passing.
When will I get my message from the spiritual
realm?
Maybe I'll see one when I spread your ashes.
I keep looking out at the big elm.
I will have to grab my rosaries and take the
helm.

Unfair

16

It seems so unfair.
You couldn't even imagine my despair.
So starts the mourning.
The best thing anyone can do is live and hope.
Even when the heart is burning.

Grief Is A Ride

Grief is a ride you don't get off of.
It changes and morphs.
It demands your attention,
like some kind of force.
Grief keeps you up all night.
It takes away your appetite.
It makes you irate.
Grief makes you
Contemplate every decision,
that you have ever made.

No Sleep

18

No sleep at night; I am devouring the dark.
Remembering my father,
his Parkinson's tremors and waning mind.
This can't be the same man who taught us tai chi
in the park.
He fought cancer for twenty years. Am I
supposed to be grateful and wipe my tears?

What Has Changed The Most

19

What has changed the most is my appreciation
for family heirlooms and stories.
Then there are all the photos, especially from
your younger days of glory,
Your sentimental side that had you save and
collect everything.
Even flowers that grew on your childhood street.
There will be no more wafts of your cologne.
No more birthday messages on my phone.
No more homemade holiday cards sent to me
from my Dad.
There will be just a rock at the graveyard.

If This Were Your Memoir

If this were your memoir, it would start with your ancestors in Portugal. Then describe your parents, Alda and Joseph, and mention you being one of five.
It would be anything but dull. Eventually, it would get to everyone throwing the wedding rice.
You became the father of three girls.
That marriage ran its course.
You met someone new and eventually went back to school.
You would have to wait for laws to change to get something borrowed new and blue.
It took over forty years, but your big day finally arrived.
You and Paul made your vows.
You both felt so alive.
Same-sex marriage should have always been allowed.

Paternal Orphan

21

I am now a paternal orphan.
The sorrow still comes.
As this is my new reality,
I must get a grip.
I will forever miss this lineal kinship.

www.ingramcontent.com/pod-product-compliance
Lightning Source LLC
La Vergne TN
LVHW021335200726
843509LV00014B/2543